# Trading With Momentum Indicators:

Momentum Oscillator, OsMA, Accelerator Oscillator, Market Facilitation Index

Volume & Momentum Series

While every precaution has been taken in the preparation of this book, the publisher assumes no responsibility for errors or omissions, or for damages resulting from the use of the information contained herein.

Additionally, Smart Money is not a registered financial advisor and no information in this publication should be viewed as trade recommendations or investment advice.

Trading With Momentum Indicators
**First edition 2024.**
Copyright © 2024 Smart Money.
Written by Smart Money.

# Index

| | |
|---|---|
| **Foreword** | **5** |
| The Momentum Oscillator Introduction | 7 |
| Momentum Oscillator Strategy #1 | 12 |
| Momentum Oscillator Strategy #2 | 16 |
| The OsMA (Oscillator of Moving Averages) | 21 |
| OsMA Trading Strategy | 25 |
| Accelerator Oscillator (AC) Introduction | 29 |
| Accelerator Oscillator (AC) Further Explained | 32 |
| Accelerator Oscillator (AC) Strategy #1 | 37 |
| Accelerator Oscillator (AC) Strategy #2 | 42 |
| Accelerator Oscillator (AC) Combinations | 47 |
| Accelerator Oscillator (AC) Backtesting | 49 |
| Accelerator Oscillator (AC) Optimization | 51 |
| Market Facilitation Index (MFI) Introduction | 58 |
| Market Facilitation Index Further Explained | 62 |
| Market Facilitation Index (MFI) Strategy #1 | 67 |
| Market Facilitation Index (MFI) Strategy #2 | 72 |
| Special Section: Combining Momentum & Volume | 77 |
| Volume as Confirmation of Momentum Breakouts | 86 |
| Momentum Divergence with Volume Context | 94 |
| Volume Climax vs Momentum Exhaustion | 102 |
| Pullbacks: Momentum Reset with Volume Contraction | 110 |
| Trend Strength: Sustained Momentum with Stable Volume | 118 |
| False Momentum Signals and Volume Disconfirmation | 126 |

| | |
|---|---|
| Momentum Regime Shifts Confirmed by Volume Rotation | 134 |
| Momentum with Volume Confirmation | 143 |
| The Integrated Execution Framework | 152 |
| Volume & Momentum Series | 161 |

# Foreword

Unlock the power of technical analysis with *Momentum Trading Indicators for Technical Analysis*. This easy to use guide delves into four of the most essential oscillators for any trader's toolkit: the Momentum Oscillator, OsMA, Accelerator Oscillator, and the Market Facilitation Index. Designed for both novice and experienced traders, this book provides clear, in-depth explanations of how these indicators work and, more importantly, how to use them to improve your trading strategy.

Explore the key principles behind each oscillator, learn how to interpret signals for market entry and exit points, and discover strategies.

Whether you're looking to sharpen your skills in identifying trends, timing market moves, or refining your technical analysis techniques, this book is your resource for mastering the momentum-driven trading. Perfect for day traders and swing traders interested in optimizing their trading performance using some of the most dynamic Momentum oscillators.

**SMART MONEY**

Smart Money Publishing

# The Momentum Oscillator Introduction

*Momentum is a measure of the rate of change of a security's price, and the oscillator helps traders identify when momentum is increasing or decreasing.*

*It's calculated by subtracting the security's price a certain number of periods ago from its current price, then dividing it by the number of periods. This creates an oscillator that fluctuates above and below a zero line.*

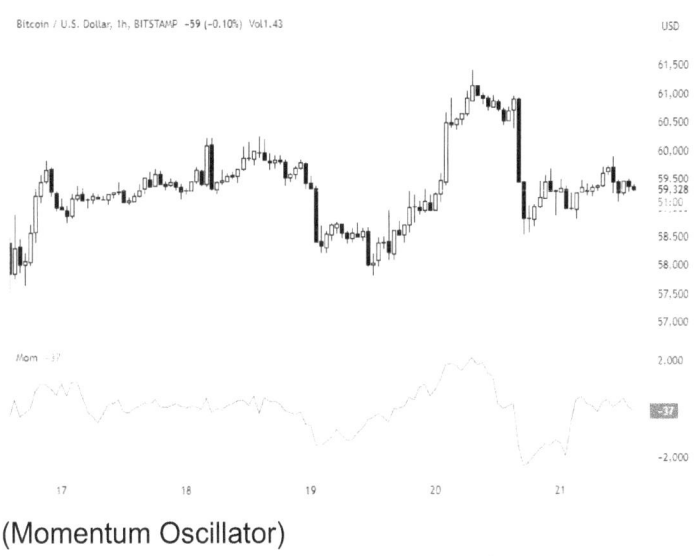

(Momentum Oscillator)

*This indicator is particularly useful for trend-following strategies, as it helps traders identify and capitalize on strong trends.*

## Calculation

The Momentum Oscillator is calculated using the following formula:

Momentum = (Current Price - Price X periods ago) / X

## Where:

- Current Price is the current market price of the security
- Price X periods ago is the market price of the security X periods ago
- X is the number of periods used in the calculation

For example, if the current price of a stock is $50 and the price 14 days ago was $45, the 14-period Momentum Oscillator would be:

Momentum = ($50 - $45) / 14 = 0.3571

## Interpretation

The Momentum Oscillator fluctuates above and below a zero line. When the oscillator is above zero, it indicates that the security's price is higher than it was X periods ago, suggesting upward momentum. Conversely, when it's below zero, it indicates downward momentum.
The oscillator's value can also be interpreted as follows:

- High positive values indicate strong upward momentum

- Low negative values indicate strong downward momentum

- Values near zero indicate little to no momentum

**Crossovers**

Traders watch for crossovers above or below the zero line, as these can signal potential buy or sell opportunities:

- Bullish crossover: When the oscillator crosses above the zero line, it may indicate a potential buy signal, as momentum is shifting from negative to positive.

- Bearish crossover: When the oscillator crosses below the zero line, it may indicate a potential sell signal, as momentum is shifting from positive to negative.

**Divergences**

Divergences between the oscillator and the security's price action can also be significant:

**Bullish divergence:** When the price is making new lows but the oscillator is failing to reach new lows, it may indicate a weakening of downward momentum and a potential buy signal.

**Bearish divergence:** When the price is making new highs but the oscillator is failing to reach new highs, it may indicate a weakening of upward momentum and a potential sell signal.

## Settings

The number of periods (X) used in the calculation can be adjusted to suit different trading strategies:

- Short-term momentum: Using a shorter period (e.g., 10 days) highlights short-term momentum and is more sensitive to price changes.

- Long-term momentum: Using a longer period (e.g., 50 days) reveals longer-term trends and is less sensitive to short-term price fluctuations.

## Combination with other indicators

Traders often use the Momentum Oscillator in conjunction with other indicators, such as:

- Moving Averages: To confirm trend direction and identify potential buy or sell signals.

- Relative Strength Index (RSI): To identify overbought or oversold conditions and potential reversals.
- Bollinger Bands: To identify volatility and potential breakouts.

**Trading Strategies**

The Momentum Oscillator can be used in various trading strategies, including:

- Trend-following: Buying securities with strong upward momentum and selling those with strong downward momentum.

- Mean reversion: Buying securities with low momentum and selling those with high momentum, expecting prices to revert to their mean.

- Range trading: Buying securities with low momentum and selling those with high momentum within an established range.

*In conclusion, the Momentum Trading Oscillator is a powerful tool for traders to gauge momentum and identify potential trading opportunities.*

*By understanding how to calculate and interpret the oscillator, traders can make more informed decisions and develop effective trading strategies.*

# Momentum Oscillator Strategy #1

Here's an example of a trading strategy using the Momentum Oscillator:

(Momentum Oscillator + 200 MA)

**Strategy** - Trend-Following with Momentum Confirmation

**Objective** - To capture strong trends in securities while minimizing false signals.

**Indicators:**

- 50-period Momentum Oscillator (MO)
- 200-period Moving Average (MA)

**Entry Rules:**

- Long (Buy) Signal:
    - MO crosses above zero
    - MO is above its 10-period MA
    - Price is above 200-period MA

- Short (Sell) Signal:
    - MO crosses below zero
    - MO is below its 10-period MA
    - Price is below 200-period MA

**Exit Rules:**

- Long (Sell) Exit:
    - MO crosses below zero
    - Price touches or breaks below 200-period MA

- Short (Cover) Exit:
    - MO crosses above zero
    - Price touches or breaks above 200-period MA

**Stop-Loss:**

- Set stop-loss at 5% below entry price for long positions
- Set stop-loss at 5% above entry price for short positions

## Example

Suppose we're trading a stock with the following data:
- Current Price: $60
- 50-period MO: 0.5 (above zero)
- 10-period MO MA: 0.2
- 200-period MA: $55

Since the MO is above zero, above its 10-period MA, and the price is above the 200-period MA, we enter a long position at $60.

## Trade Management

- As the price moves up, we trail our stop-loss to $57 (5% below entry price)
- If the MO crosses below zero or the price touches the 200-period MA, we exit the trade

## Rationale

This strategy combines the Momentum Oscillator with a moving average to confirm trend direction. By requiring the MO to be above its 10-period MA, we ensure that momentum is strong and sustainable. The 200-period MA provides a longer-term perspective on trend direction. By setting a stop-loss at 5% below entry price, we limit potential losses.

**Advantages**

- Captures strong trends with momentum confirmation
- Minimizes false signals using multiple indicators
- Provides clear entry and exit rules

**Disadvantages**

- May miss some trading opportunities due to strict entry rules
- Requires monitoring of multiple indicators

*This is just one example of a trading strategy using the Momentum Oscillator. Traders can modify and adapt this strategy to suit their individual needs and market conditions.*

# Momentum Oscillator Strategy #2

Here is another example of a trading strategy using the Momentum Oscillator:

(Momentum Oscillator + 50 MA + 200 MA)

**Strategy** - Momentum + Trend

**Objective** - To capture strong trends in securities while minimizing false signals and maximizing profits.

**Indicators:**

- 50-period Momentum Oscillator (MO)
- 200-period Moving Average (MA)
- 14-period Relative Strength Index (RSI)
- Bollinger Bands (20,2)

**Entry Rules:**

- Long (Buy) Signal:
    - MO crosses above zero
    - MO is above its 10-period MA
    - Price is above 200-period MA
    - RSI is below 50
    - Price touches or breaks above upper Bollinger Band

- Short (Sell) Signal:
    - MO crosses below zero
    - MO is below its 10-period MA
    - Price is below 200-period MA
    - RSI is above 50
    - Price touches or breaks below lower Bollinger Band

**Exit Rules:**

- Long (Sell) Exit:
    - MO crosses below zero
    - Price touches or breaks below 200-period MA
    - RSI reaches 70

- Short (Cover) Exit:
    - MO crosses above zero
    - Price touches or breaks above 200-period MA
    - RSI reaches 30

**Stop-Loss:**

- Set stop-loss at 5% below entry price for long positions
- Set stop-loss at 5% above entry price for short positions

**Example**

Suppose we're trading a stock with the following data:

- Current Price: $60
- 50-period MO: 0.5 (above zero)
- 10-period MO MA: 0.2
- 200-period MA: $55
- 14-period RSI: 40
- Bollinger Bands: Upper Band $62, Lower Band $58

Since the MO is above zero, above its 10-period MA, price is above 200-period MA, RSI is below 50, and price touches upper Bollinger Band, we enter a long position at $60.

**Trade Management**

- As the price moves up, we trail our stop-loss to $57 (5% below entry price)
- If the MO crosses below zero or price touches 200-period MA, we exit the trade

## Rationale

This strategy combines the Momentum Oscillator with a moving average, RSI, and Bollinger Bands to confirm trend direction, momentum, and volatility. By requiring the MO to be above its 10-period MA, we ensure that momentum is strong and sustainable. The 200-period MA provides a longer-term perspective on trend direction. The RSI helps us avoid overbought conditions, while Bollinger Bands provide a volatility filter.

## Advantages

- Captures strong trends with momentum confirmation
- Minimizes false signals using multiple indicators
- Provides clear entry and exit rules
- Manages risk with stop-loss and position sizing

## Disadvantages

- May miss some trading opportunities due to strict entry rules
- Requires monitoring of multiple indicators

*This is just one example of a trading strategy using the Momentum Oscillator. Traders can modify and adapt this strategy to suit their individual needs and market conditions.*

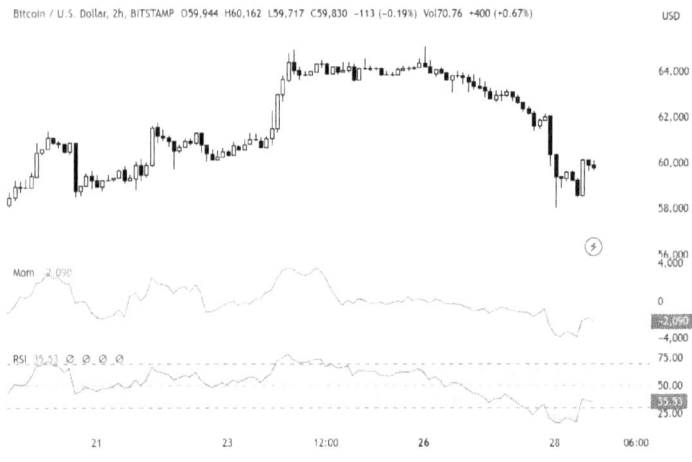

(Momentum Oscillator + RSI)

(Momentum Oscillator + Bollinger Bands)

# The OsMA (Oscillator of Moving Averages)

*The OsMA (Oscillator of Moving Averages) is a technical indicator and extension of the MACD oscillator that measures the difference between two moving averages, providing traders with valuable insights into market momentum and direction.*

**(OsMA - Oscillator of Moving Averages)**

**Calculation:**

OsMA = MACD - Signal Line

*MACD (Moving Average Convergence Divergence):*

- *Fast EMA (12-period)*
- *Slow EMA (26-period)*
- *MACD = Fast EMA - Slow EMA*

**Signal Line:**

- 9-period EMA of MACD

**Interpretation:**

- **OsMA above zero line:** Bullish momentum, indicating a potential uptrend

- **OsMA below zero line:** Bearish momentum, indicating a potential downtrend

- **OsMA crossing zero line:** Indicates a change in momentum, potentially signaling a trend reversal

**Usage:**

1. _Identify Momentum:_ Look for OsMA to cross above or below the zero line, indicating a change in momentum.

2. _Divergence:_ Identify divergences between OsMA and price, potentially signaling a trend reversal.

3. _Confirm Trends:_ Use OsMA to confirm trend direction indicated by other indicators.

## Advantages:

1. Simple and Easy to Understand: OsMA is a straightforward indicator to interpret.

2. Effective in Determining Momentum and Direction: OsMA provides valuable insights into market momentum and direction.

3. Can be Used in Conjunction with Other Technical Indicators: OsMA complements other indicators, providing a comprehensive market view.

## Limitations:

1. _Lagging Indicator:_ OsMA reacts to price movements after they occur, potentially leading to delayed signals.

2. _Can Produce False Signals in Volatile Markets:_ OsMA may generate false signals in highly volatile markets, requiring additional confirmation.

## Strategy

1. _Long Entry:_ OsMA crosses above zero line, price breaks above resistance, and RSI is above 50.

2. _Short Entry:_ OsMA crosses below zero line, price breaks below support, and RSI is below 50.

3. _Stop-Loss:_ Set at 10-15 pips above/below entry price.

4. _Take-Profit:_ Set at 20-30 pips above/below entry price.

**Example**

- EUR/USD, 1-hour chart

- OsMA crosses above zero line, price breaks above resistance, and RSI is above 50

- Entry price: 1.1050

- Stop-loss: 1.1040

- Take-profit: 1.1070

By incorporating OsMA into your trading strategy, you can gain valuable insights into market momentum and direction, potentially improving your trading performance. However, always test and refine strategies before live trading.

# OsMA Trading Strategy

Here's an example trading strategy using the OsMA trading oscillator:

**(OsMA + MA 50)**

**Strategy: OsMA Momentum Breakout Strategy**

**Indicators:**

- OsMA (14-period)
- Moving Average (50-period)
- RSI (14-period)
- Bollinger Bands (20, 2)

**Long Entry:**

1. OsMA crosses above zero line
2. Price breaks above 50-period moving average
3. RSI is above 50
4. Price touches or breaks above the upper Bollinger Band
5. Entry price: Highest high of the last 5 bars
6. Stop-loss: 10 pips below entry price
7. Take-profit: 20 pips above entry price

**Short Entry:**

1. OsMA crosses below zero line
2. Price breaks below 50-period moving average
3. RSI is below 50
4. Price touches or breaks below the lower Bollinger Band
5. Entry price: Lowest low of the last 5 bars
6. Stop-loss: 10 pips above entry price
7. Take-profit: 20 pips below entry price

**Additional Rules:**

- Only enter trades in the direction of the trend (moving average)

- Use RSI to confirm momentum

- Use Bollinger Bands to confirm volatility and trend strength

- Adjust stop-loss and take-profit levels based on market volatility

(OsMA + Bollinger Bands)

**Example:**

- EUR/USD, 1-hour chart

- OsMA crosses above zero line, price breaks above 50-period moving average, RSI is above 50, and price touches upper Bollinger Band

- Entry price: 1.1050

- Stop-loss: 1.1040

- Take-profit: 1.1070

(OsMA + RSI)

**Conclusion**

This strategy uses OsMA to identify momentum, moving average to confirm trend direction, RSI to confirm momentum, and Bollinger Bands to confirm volatility and trend strength.

By combining these indicators, traders can potentially profit from momentum breakouts and trend continuations. However, always test and refine strategies before live trading.

# Bill Williams Accelerator Oscillator (AC) Introduction

The Bill Williams Accelerator Oscillator (AC) is a technical analysis indicator developed by Bill Williams, a renowned trader and author. It's a momentum indicator that helps identify potential trend reversals, measure market momentum and spot trading opportunities. Here's an introductory overview:

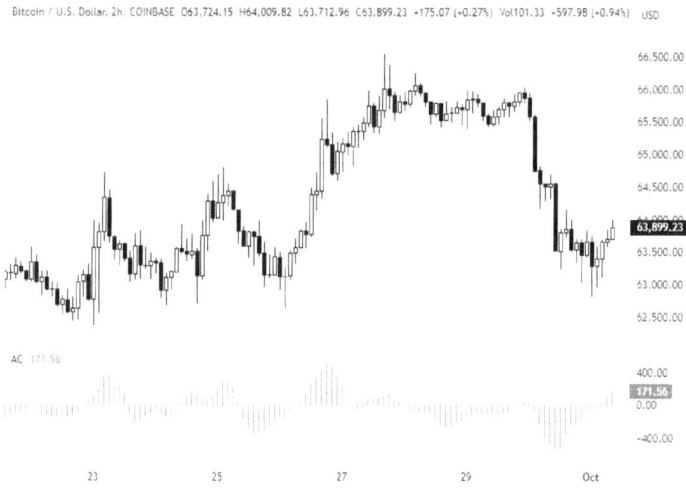

(Bill Williams Accelerator Oscillator - AC)

**What does the Accelerator Oscillator measure?**

The AC indicator measures the difference between the driving force (momentum) and the price movement. It compares the current price movement to its previous state, highlighting the acceleration or deceleration of the market.

**\*Key components:\***

1. \*Histogram\*: The AC indicator displays a histogram with red and green bars, indicating the difference between the driving force and price movement.

2. \*Zero Line\*: The zero line serves as a benchmark, separating positive and negative values.

3. \*Color change\*: Color changes on the histogram indicate a change in momentum direction.

**\*Interpretation:\***

1. \*Bullish signals\*: Green bars above the zero line indicate increasing upward momentum.

2. \*Bearish signals\*: Red bars below the zero line indicate increasing downward momentum.

3. \*Divergences\*: When the AC histogram diverges from the price movement, it may signal a potential trend reversal.

4. \*Zero line crossings\*: When the histogram crosses the zero line, it indicates a change in momentum direction.

**Trading strategies:**

1. *Long positions*: Enter when the histogram turns green and crosses above the zero line.

2. *Short positions*: Enter when the histogram turns red and crosses below the zero line.

3. *Stop-loss*: Set stops based on previous swing highs/lows or AC histogram extremes.

**Limitations:**

1. *False signals*: The AC can generate false signals in volatile or ranging markets.

2. *Confirmation*: Use the AC in combination with other indicators or analysis techniques to confirm trading decisions.

The Bill Williams Accelerator Oscillator is a valuable tool for traders seeking to identify momentum shifts and potential trend reversals. However, it's essential to understand its limitations and combine it with other forms of analysis for more effective trading decisions.

# Bill Williams Accelerator Oscillator (AC) Further Explained

Here's a detailed and advanced explanation of the Bill Williams Accelerator Oscillator (AC) trading indicator:

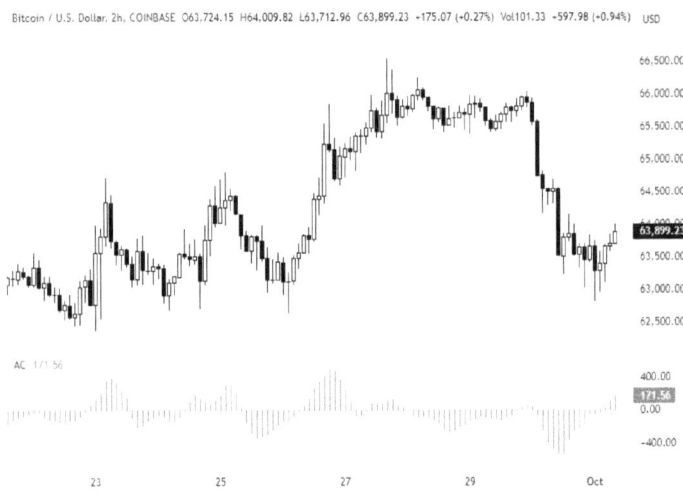

(Bill Williams Accelerator Oscillator - AC)

*Mathematical Calculation:*

The Accelerator Oscillator is calculated using the following formula:

AC = AO - AO(-1)

Where:

- AC = Accelerator Oscillator
- AO = Awesome Oscillator (another Bill Williams indicator)
- AO(-1) = Previous bar's Awesome Oscillator value

**The Awesome Oscillator (AO) is calculated as:**

AO = SMA(MedPrice, 5) - SMA(MedPrice, 34)

Where:

- MedPrice = (High + Low) / 2 (Median Price)
- SMA = Simple Moving Average

**\*Interpretation:\***

1. *Histogram Direction*: The direction of the histogram bars indicates the momentum direction.
    - Upward-moving green bars: Increasing upward momentum.
    - Downward-moving red bars: Increasing downward momentum.

2. *Zero Line Crossings*: When the histogram crosses the zero line, it indicates a change in momentum direction.
    - Cross above zero: Potential bullish reversal.
    - Cross below zero: Potential bearish reversal.

3. *Divergences*: When the AC histogram diverges from the price movement, it may signal a potential trend reversal.
   - Bullish divergence: AC histogram makes higher lows while price makes lower lows.
   - Bearish divergence: AC histogram makes lower highs while price makes higher highs.

4. *Color Changes*: Color changes on the histogram indicate a change in momentum direction.
   - Green to red: Potential bearish reversal.
   - Red to green: Potential bullish reversal.

5. *Extreme Values*: AC values exceeding ±30-40 levels indicate overbought/oversold conditions.

**Advanced Trading Strategies:**

1. *AC Zero Line Crossover Strategy*: Enter long/short positions when the AC histogram crosses above/below the zero line.

2. *AC Divergence Strategy*: Enter long/short positions when divergence occurs between AC histogram and price movement.

3. *AC Extreme Values Strategy*: Enter long/short positions when AC values reach extreme levels (±30-40).

4. *AC Histogram Reversal Strategy*: Enter long/short positions when the histogram changes direction (green to red or red to green).

5. *Combination Strategies*: Combine AC with other indicators (e.g., Fractals, Alligator, or RSI) for confirmation.

**Additional Insights:**

1. *Momentum Confirmation*: Use AC to confirm momentum changes indicated by other indicators.

2. *Trend Strength*: AC helps evaluate trend strength; strong trends have consistent histogram direction.

3. *Market Context*: Consider market context; AC performs better in trending markets.

4. *Time Frame*: Optimize AC performance by adjusting time frames; shorter TFs for scalping, longer TFs for swing trading.

5. *Stop-Loss Placement*: Use AC extremes or previous swing highs/lows to set stop-loss levels.

**\*Limitations and Considerations:\***

1. \*False Signals\*: AC can generate false signals in volatile or ranging markets.

2. \*Lag\*: AC, like other momentum indicators, can lag price movement.

3. \*Over-Reliance\*: Avoid relying solely on AC; combine with other analysis techniques.

4. \*Parameter Optimization\*: Experiment with different SMA lengths and time frames to optimize AC performance.

By understanding the advanced aspects of the Bill Williams Accelerator Oscillator, traders can refine their trading strategies and improve their market analysis.

# Bill Williams Accelerator Oscillator (AC) Strategy #1

Here is an example of a trading strategy using the Bill Williams Accelerator Oscillator (AC) trading indicator:

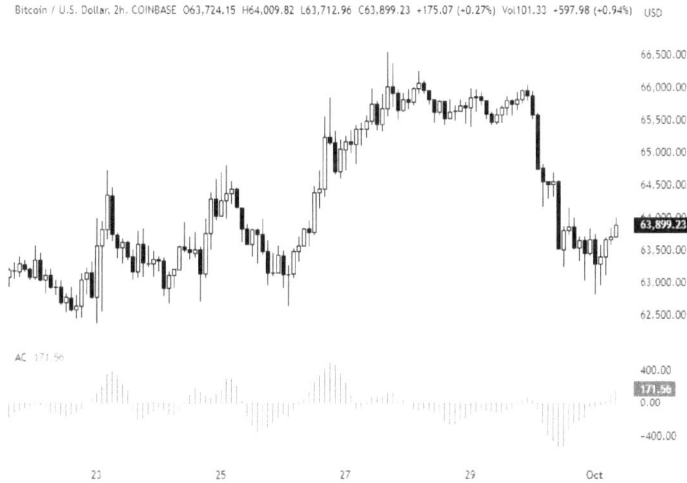

(Bill Williams Accelerator Oscillator - AC)

**Strategy:** AC-Based Mean Reversion Strategy

**Objective:** Identify potential mean reversion opportunities using the AC indicator.

**Setup:**

1. Time Frame: 4-hour or daily chart
2. Currency Pair: Any liquid pair (e.g., EUR/USD, GBP/USD, USD/JPY)
3. Indicators:
    - Bill Williams Accelerator Oscillator (AC)
    - 50-period Simple Moving Average (SMA50)
    - Relative Strength Index (RSI, 14-period)

**Long Entry Rules:**

1. Price is below SMA50.
2. AC histogram is below -30 level (oversold).
3. RSI is below 30 level (oversold).
4. AC histogram changes color from red to green.
5. Buy at the close of the candle.

**Short Entry Rules:**

1. Price is above SMA50.
2. AC histogram is above 30 level (overbought).
3. RSI is above 70 level (overbought).
4. AC histogram changes color from green to red.
5. Sell at the close of the candle.

**Exit Rules:**

1. Set stop-loss at 20-30 pips above/below entry price.
2. Take profit when AC histogram reaches extreme levels (±40) or RSI reaches 50 level.

3. Optional: Trail stop-loss using AC histogram extremes or previous swing highs/lows.

**Rationale:**

1. SMA50 provides trend direction context.
2. AC histogram extreme levels (-30 or 30) indicate overbought/oversold conditions.
3. RSI confirmation reinforces mean reversion potential.
4. Color change on AC histogram indicates momentum shift.
5. Mean reversion strategy aims to capitalize on price returning to its mean value.

**Additional Considerations:**

1. Filtering: Use ADX (Average Directional Index) to filter out weak trends.
2. Timing: Optimize strategy performance by adjusting time frames and AC/RSI parameters.
3. Risk Management: Adjust stop-loss and position sizing according to market volatility.
4. Confirmation: Combine with other indicators (e.g., Fractals, Alligator) for added confirmation.

(Accelerator Oscillator + 50MA)

(Accelerator Oscillator + RSI)

**Example:**

EUR/USD 4-hour chart:

- Price: 1.1000
- SMA50: 1.1050
- AC: -35 (oversold)
- RSI: 25 (oversold)
- AC histogram changes color from red to green

Buy at 1.1000, stop-loss at 1.0980, take profit at 1.1100 (AC reaches 40 level)

**Backtesting:**

Backtest this strategy using historical data to evaluate its performance and refine parameters.

**Limitations:**

1. False signals in trending markets
2. Lag in AC and RSI indicators
3. Over-reliance on mean reversion assumption

By combining the Bill Williams Accelerator Oscillator with other indicators and techniques, traders can create robust trading strategies tailored to their market analysis and risk management preferences.

# Bill Williams Accelerator Oscillator (AC) Strategy #2

Here's another example of a trading strategy using the Bill Williams Accelerator Oscillator (AC) trading indicator:

(Bill Williams Accelerator Oscillator)

**Strategy: AC-Based Trend Continuation Strategy**

**Objective:** Identify and ride trending markets using the AC indicator.

**Setup:**

1. Time Frame: 4-hour or daily chart
2. Currency Pair: Any liquid pair (e.g., EUR/USD, GBP/USD, USD/JPY)
3. Indicators:
   - Bill Williams Accelerator Oscillator (AC)
   - 100-period Simple Moving Average (SMA100)
   - Fractals (Bill Williams)

**Long Entry Rules:**

1. Price is above SMA100.
2. AC histogram is above zero.
3. AC histogram is increasing (green bars).
4. Fractal buy signal (green fractal below price).
5. Buy at the close of the candle.

Short Entry Rules:

1. Price is below SMA100.
2. AC histogram is below zero.
3. AC histogram is decreasing (red bars).
4. Fractal sell signal (red fractal above price).
5. Sell at the close of the candle.

**Exit Rules:**

1. Set stop-loss at 20-30 pips above/below entry price.
2. Take profit when AC histogram reaches extreme levels (±40) or Fractal reversal signal.

3. Optional: Trail stop-loss using AC histogram extremes or previous swing highs/lows.

**Rationale:**

1. SMA100 provides trend direction context.
2. AC histogram above/below zero indicates upward/downward momentum.
3. Increasing/decreasing AC histogram confirms trend continuation.
4. Fractals provide additional confirmation for entry/exit.

**Additional Considerations:**

1. Filter: Use ADX (Average Directional Index) to filter out weak trends.
2. Timing: Optimize strategy performance by adjusting time frames and AC/Fractal parameters.
3. Risk Management: Adjust stop-loss and position sizing according to market volatility.

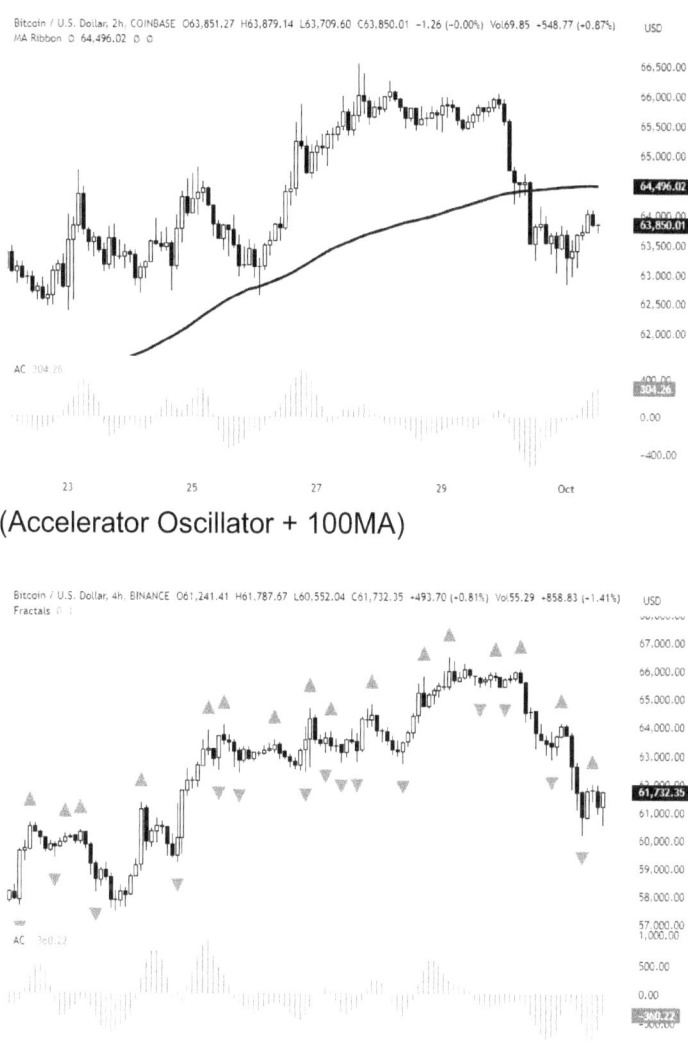

(Accelerator Oscillator + 100MA)

(Accelerator Oscillator + Williams Fractals)

**Example:**

EUR/USD 4-hour chart:

- Price: 1.1050
- SMA100: 1.1000
- AC: 20 (above zero, increasing)
- Fractal: Green fractal below price

Buy at 1.1050, stop-loss at 1.1020, take profit at 1.1150 (AC reaches 40 level)

# Bill Williams Accelerator Oscillator (AC) Strategy Combinations

Here are some additional combinations of the Bill Williams Accelerator Oscillator (AC) with other indicators or strategies:

### Combination 1: AC + RSI + Bollinger Bands

- Long entry: AC above zero, RSI below 30, price touches lower Bollinger Band.
- Short entry: AC below zero, RSI above 70, price touches upper Bollinger Band.

### Combination 2: AC + Moving Averages + Stochastic Oscillator

- Long entry: AC above zero, price above 50-period MA, Stochastic Oscillator below 20.
- Short entry: AC below zero, price below 50-period MA, Stochastic Oscillator above 80.

### Combination 3: AC + Fractals + Ichimoku Cloud

- Long entry: AC above zero, Fractal buy signal, price above Ichimoku Cloud.
- Short entry: AC below zero, Fractal sell signal, price below Ichimoku Cloud.

**Additional Indicators:**

- Volume indicators (e.g., Volume RSI, On Balance Volume).
- Momentum indicators (e.g., Momentum, Rate of Change).
- Trend indicators (e.g., ADX, Super Trend).

**Optimization Tips:**

- Use walk-forward optimization to refine parameters.
- Test different time frames and currency pairs.
- Incorporate risk management techniques (e.g., position sizing, stop-loss).

By combining the AC indicator with other technical analysis tools, traders can create robust trading strategies tailored to their market analysis and risk management preferences.

# Bill Williams Accelerator Oscillator (AC) Backtesting & Optimization

Here's a detailed guide on backtesting and optimizing the AC-Based Mean Reversion Strategy:

**Backtesting:**

1. Choose a trading platform or software (e.g., MetaTrader, TradingView, Python libraries like Backtrader or Zipline).
2. Select historical data (e.g., 1-year, 5-year) for the chosen currency pair.
3. Set up the strategy parameters:
    - AC period
    - RSI period
    - SMA50 period
    - Stop-loss and take-profit levels
4. Run the backtest to evaluate performance metrics:
    - Profit/Loss
    - Return on Account (ROA)
    - Drawdown
    - Sharpe Ratio
    - Number of trades

**Optimization:**

1. Identify key parameters to optimize:
   - AC threshold levels (e.g., -30 to -40)
   - RSI threshold levels (e.g., 20 to 30)
   - SMA50 period (e.g., 50 to 200)
   - Stop-loss and take-profit levels
2. Use optimization techniques:
   - Grid search
   - Random search
   - Genetic algorithms
   - Walk-forward optimization
3. Evaluate optimized parameters using metrics like:
   - Profit/Loss
   - Return on Account (ROA)
   - Drawdown
   - Sharpe Ratio

**Walk-Forward Optimization:**

1. Divide historical data into training and testing periods.
2. Optimize parameters on training period.
3. Evaluate performance on testing period.
4. Repeat steps 2-3 for each walk-forward period.

By backtesting and optimizing the AC-Based Mean Reversion Strategy, traders can refine the approach to better suit market conditions and improve overall performance.

# Bill Williams Accelerator Oscillator (AC) Strategy Optimization

Optimization is a critical step in refining the AC-Based Mean Reversion Strategy to achieve better performance. Here's a detailed explanation of the optimization process:

**Optimization Goals**

1. Maximize return on account (ROA)
2. Minimize drawdown
3. Improve Sharpe Ratio
4. Increase profit factor

**Optimization Parameters**

1. AC period (5-30)
2. RSI period (5-30)
3. SMA50 period (20-200)
4. Stop-loss levels (10-50 pips)
5. Take-profit levels (10-50 pips)
6. Position sizing (1-5%)
7. Leverage (1-10)

## Optimization Techniques

1. Grid Search: Exhaustive search of all parameter combinations
2. Random Search: Random sampling of parameter combinations
3. Genetic Algorithms: Evolutionary optimization using selection, crossover, and mutation
4. Walk-Forward Optimization: Optimization on rolling time windows
5. Hyperparameter Tuning: Bayesian optimization using libraries like Hyperopt or Optuna

## Optimization Metrics

1. Profit/Loss
2. Return on Account (ROA)
3. Drawdown
4. Sharpe Ratio
5. Profit Factor
6. Number of trades
7. Win/Loss ratio

## Optimization Tools

1. Backtrader (Python)
2. Hyperopt (Python)
3. Optuna (Python)
4. QuantConnect (C#)
5. Quantopian (Python)

## Example Optimization Code (Python using Hyperopt)

```python
import hyperopt

def optimize_ac_params():
    space = {
        'ac_period': hyperopt.hp.quniform('ac_period', 5, 30, 1),
        'rsi_period': hyperopt.hp.quniform('rsi_period', 5, 30, 1),
        'sma_period': hyperopt.hp.quniform('sma_period', 20, 200, 10)
    }

    def evaluate_params(params):
        # Run backtest with params
        cerebro = bt.Cerebro()
        cerebro.addstrategy(AC_Mean_Reversion, ac_period=params['ac_period'],
                    rsi_period=params['rsi_period'], sma_period=params['sma_period'])
        cerebro.run()
        return -cerebro.broker.getvalue()  # Minimize negative equity

    best = hyperopt.fmin(evaluate_params, space, algo=hyperopt.tpe.suggest, max_evals=50)
    return best
```

## Optimization Considerations

1. Overfitting: Monitor performance across multiple time periods
2. Curve-fitting: Avoid optimizing parameters for a single time period
3. Survivorship bias: Ensure data includes delisted or bankrupt instruments
4. Computational resources: Balance optimization complexity with computational resources

By optimizing the AC-Based Mean Reversion Strategy using these techniques and tools, traders can refine the approach to better suit market conditions and improve overall performance.

# Bill Williams Accelerator Oscillator (AC) Strategy Backtesting

Backtesting the AC-Based Mean Reversion Strategy

Backtesting is a crucial step in evaluating the performance of the AC-Based Mean Reversion Strategy. Here's a detailed explanation of the backtesting process:

**Backtesting Platforms**

Choose a suitable backtesting platform, such as:

1. MetaTrader (MT4/MT5)
2. TradingView (PineScript)
3. Python libraries (Backtrader, Zipline, Catalyst)
4. Commercial platforms (QuantConnect, Quantopian)

**Data Requirements**

1. Historical data for the chosen currency pair (e.g., EUR/USD)

2. Time frame: 1-minute, 5-minute, 1-hour, 4-hour, or daily

3. Data frequency: Tick, minute, or daily data
4. Data sources: Reliable data providers (e.g., Quandl, Alpha Vantage)

**Backtesting Parameters**

1. Strategy parameters:
    - AC period
    - RSI period
    - SMA50 period
    - Stop-loss and take-profit levels
2. Initial capital
3. Risk management settings (e.g., position sizing, leverage)
4. Trading costs (e.g., spreads, commissions)

**Backtesting Process**

1. Load historical data into the backtesting platform
2. Set up the strategy parameters and initial capital
3. Run the backtest for the specified time period
4. Evaluate performance metrics:
    - Profit/Loss
    - Return on Account (ROA)
    - Drawdown
    - Sharpe Ratio
    - Number of trades
    - Win/Loss ratio
5. Visualize equity curves and trade distributions

## Backtesting Considerations

1. Survivorship bias: Ensure data includes delisted or bankrupt instruments
2. Look-ahead bias: Avoid using future data in the backtest
3. Overfitting: Monitor performance across multiple time periods
4. Curve-fitting: Avoid optimizing parameters for a single time period

# Bill Williams Market Facilitation Index (MFI) Introduction

The Bill Williams Market Facilitation Index (MFI) is a technical analysis indicator developed by Bill Williams, a renowned trader and author. It measures the efficiency of price movement by analyzing the relationship between price changes and volume.

(Bill Williams Market Facilitation Index - MFI)

**Definition:**

The Market Facilitation Index is calculated by dividing the price change by the volume. This ratio indicates the "efficiency" of price movement.

**Calculation:**

MFI = (Price Change / Volume)

**Interpretation:**

1. High MFI: Efficient price movement, indicating strong market momentum.
2. Low MFI: Inefficient price movement, indicating weak market momentum.

**Key Features:**

1. Volume Confirmation: MFI confirms price movements with volume.
2. Trend Identification: MFI helps identify trends and potential reversals.

**Trading Signals:**

1. Buy Signal: MFI increases during an uptrend.
2. Sell Signal: MFI decreases during a downtrend.

**Additional Insights:**

1. MFI Divergences: Divergences between MFI and price indicate potential reversals.
2. MFI Extreme Values: Extremely high/low MFI values indicate overbought/oversold conditions.

**Limitations:**

1. False Signals: MFI can generate false signals in volatile markets.
2. Lag: MFI can lag price movement.

**Best Used With:**

1. Trend indicators (e.g., Moving Averages, Alligator)
2. Momentum indicators (e.g., RSI, Awesome Oscillator)
3. Volume indicators (e.g., Volume RSI, On Balance Volume)

**Coding Example (Python):**

```
import pandas as pd

def market_facilitation_index(prices):
    mfi = []
    for i in range(1, len(prices)):
        price_change = prices['Close'].iloc[i] - prices['Close'].iloc[i-1]
        volume = prices['Volume'].iloc[i]
        mfi.append(price_change / volume)
    return mfi

# Test Market Facilitation Index
prices = pd.read_csv("prices.csv")
mfi = market_facilitation_index(prices)
print(mfi)
```

```

By understanding the Market Facilitation Index, traders can gain valuable insights into market efficiency and make more informed trading decisions.
```

# Bill Williams Market Facilitation Index (MFI) Further Explained

Here's a detailed and advanced explanation of the Bill Williams Market Facilitation Index (MFI) trading indicator:

(Bill Williams Market Facilitation Index - MFI)

**Advanced Calculation:**

MFI = (Price Change / Volume) x (Price Change / Previous Price Change)

This modified calculation considers the rate of price change and volume, providing a more nuanced view of market efficiency.

**Additional Parameters:**

1. Volume Threshold: Minimum volume required for MFI calculation (default 1000)
2. Price Change Threshold: Minimum price change required for MFI calculation (default 0.1%)

**Indicator Components:**

1. MFI Line: Displays the Market Facilitation Index values
2. Signal Line: Displays the smoothed MFI values (e.g., 7-period moving average)
3. Histogram: Displays the difference between MFI and Signal Lines

**Trading Signals:**

1. Buy Signal: MFI Line crosses above Signal Line
2. Sell Signal: MFI Line crosses below Signal Line
3. Divergence Signal: MFI Line diverges from price movement

**Advanced Trading Strategies:**

1. MFI Trend Strategy: Buy/Sell when MFI Line is above/below Signal Line
2. MFI Reversal Strategy: Buy/Sell when MFI Line diverges from price movement

3. MFI Breakout Strategy: Buy/Sell when MFI Line breaks through previous highs/lows

**MFI Patterns:**

1. MFI Divergence: Divergence between MFI Line and price movement
2. MFI Convergence: Convergence between MFI Line and price movement
3. MFI Extreme Values: Extremely high/low MFI values indicate overbought/oversold conditions

**Combination Strategies:**

1. MFI + Alligator: Use MFI to confirm Alligator-based trade entries
2. MFI + Awesome Oscillator: Combine MFI with AO's momentum signals
3. MFI + Volume Indicators: Use MFI with volume indicators (e.g., Volume RSI, OBV)

**Optimization Tips:**

1. Adjust Volume and Price Change Thresholds
2. Use different MFI calculation periods
3. Combine MFI with other indicators for confirmation

**Limitations:**

1. False Signals: MFI can generate false signals in volatile markets
2. Lag: MFI can lag price movement

**Coding Example (Python):**

```
import pandas as pd
import numpy as np

def advanced_market_facilitation_index(prices, volume_threshold=1000, price_change_threshold=0.001):
    mfi = []
    signal = []
    for i in range(1, len(prices)):
        price_change = prices['Close'].iloc[i] - prices['Close'].iloc[i-1]
        volume = prices['Volume'].iloc[i]

        if volume > volume_threshold and abs(price_change) > price_change_threshold:
            mfi.append((price_change / volume) * (price_change / prices['Close'].iloc[i-1]))
        else:
            mfi.append(np.nan)

        signal.append(np.mean(mfi[-7:]))
```

```
    return mfi, signal

# Test Advanced Market Facilitation Index
prices = pd.read_csv("prices.csv")
mfi, signal = advanced_market_facilitation_index(prices)
print(mfi, signal)
```

By mastering the Bill Williams Market Facilitation Index, traders can refine their market analysis and identify potential trading opportunities.

# Bill Williams Market Facilitation Index (MFI) Strategy #1

Here's an example of a trading strategy using the Bill Williams Market Facilitation Index (MFI) and Envelopes trading indicators:

(Bill Williams Market Facilitation Index - MFI)

**Strategy Name:** MFI Envelopes Breakout Strategy

**Objective:** Identify potential trend continuations and reversals using MFI and Envelopes.

**Setup:**

1. Time Frame: 4-hour or daily chart
2. Currency Pair: Any liquid pair (e.g., EUR/USD, GBP/USD, USD/JPY)
3. Indicators:
    - Bill Williams Market Facilitation Index (MFI)
    - Envelopes (20-period, 10% deviation)

**Long Entry Rules:**

1. Price breaks through Upper Envelope.
2. MFI Line is above Signal Line.
3. MFI Value is above 0.5.

**Short Entry Rules:**
1. Price breaks through Lower Envelope.
2. MFI Line is below Signal Line.
3. MFI Value is below -0.5.

**Exit Rules:**
1. Set stop-loss at 20-30 pips above/below entry price.
2. Take profit when price reaches opposite Envelope.

**Rationale:**
1. Envelopes provide trend identification and breakout signals.
2. MFI confirms trend strength and potential reversals.

(MFI + Envelopes)

**Example:**

EUR/USD 4-hour chart:

- Price: 1.1050
- Upper Envelope: 1.1100
- Lower Envelope: 1.1000
- MFI: 0.7 (above Signal Line)

Buy at 1.1100, stop-loss at 1.1070, take profit at 1.1200 (Lower Envelope)

**Backtesting:**

Backtest this strategy using historical data to evaluate its performance and refine parameters.
Additional Considerations:

1. Filter: Use ADX (Average Directional Index) to filter out weak trends.
2. Timing: Optimize strategy performance by adjusting time frames and Envelope parameters.
3. Risk Management: Adjust stop-loss and position sizing according to market volatility.

**Combination Strategies:**

1. MFI + Alligator: Use MFI to confirm Alligator-based trade entries.
2. Envelopes + RSI: Combine Envelopes with RSI's overbought/oversold signals.

**Python Code Example:**

```
import pandas as pd
import numpy as np

def mfi_envelopes_breakout(prices):
    mfi = advanced_market_facilitation_index(prices)[0]
    envelopes = envelopes_indicator(prices, period=20, deviation=0.1)
```

```
    signals = pd.DataFrame(index=prices.index,
columns=['Buy', 'Sell'])
    signals['Buy'] = (prices['Close'] > envelopes['Upper'])
& (mfi > 0.5) & (mfi > mfi.shift(1))
    signals['Sell'] = (prices['Close'] < envelopes['Lower'])
& (mfi < -0.5) & (mfi < mfi.shift(1))

    return signals

# Test MFI Envelopes Breakout Strategy
prices = pd.read_csv("prices.csv")
signals = mfi_envelopes_breakout(prices)
print(signals)
```

By combining the Bill Williams Market Facilitation Index with Envelopes, traders can identify potential trend continuations and reversals.

# Bill Williams Market Facilitation Index (MFI) Strategy #2

Here's another example of a trading strategy using the Bill Williams Market Facilitation Index (MFI) trading indicator:

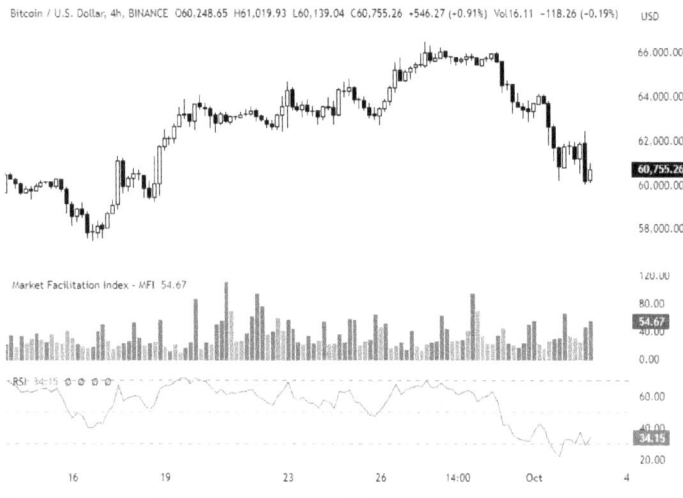

(Market Facilitation Index + RSI)

**Strategy Name:** MFI Divergence Reversal Strategy

Objective: Identify potential trend reversals using MFI divergences.

**Setup:**

1. Time Frame: 4-hour or daily chart
2. Currency Pair: Any liquid pair (e.g., EUR/USD, GBP/USD, USD/JPY)
3. Indicators:
   - Bill Williams Market Facilitation Index (MFI)
   - Relative Strength Index (RSI) (14-period)

**Long Entry Rules:**

1. Bullish MFI Divergence: MFI makes higher lows while price makes lower lows.
2. RSI Oversold: RSI falls below 30.
3. Buy at the close of the candle.

**Short Entry Rules:**

1. Bearish MFI Divergence: MFI makes lower highs while price makes higher highs.
2. RSI Overbought: RSI rises above 70.
3. Sell at the close of the candle.

**Exit Rules:**

1. Set stop-loss at 20-30 pips above/below entry price.
2. Take profit when MFI converges with price movement.

**Rationale:**

1. MFI divergences indicate potential trend reversals.
2. RSI confirms overbought/oversold conditions.

**Example:**

EUR/USD 4-hour chart:

- Price: 1.1050 (lower low)
- MFI: 0.8 (higher low)
- RSI: 25 (oversold)

Buy at 1.1050, stop-loss at 1.1020, take profit at 1.1150 (MFI converges with price)

**Backtesting:**

Backtest this strategy using historical data to evaluate its performance and refine parameters.

**Additional Considerations:**

1. Filter: Use ADX (Average Directional Index) to filter out weak trends.
2. Timing: Optimize strategy performance by adjusting time frames and MFI parameters.
3. Risk Management: Adjust stop-loss and position sizing according to market volatility.

**Combination Strategies:**

1. MFI + Alligator: Use MFI to confirm Alligator-based trade entries.
2. MFI + Awesome Oscillator: Combine MFI with AO's momentum signals.

**Python Code Example:**

```
import pandas as pd
import numpy as np

def mfi_divergence_reversal(prices):
    mfi = advanced_market_facilitation_index(prices)[0]
    rsi = rsi_indicator(prices, period=14)

    signals = pd.DataFrame(index=prices.index, columns=['Buy', 'Sell'])
    signals['Buy'] = (mfi > mfi.shift(1)) & (prices['Low'] < prices['Low'].shift(1)) & (rsi < 30)
    signals['Sell'] = (mfi < mfi.shift(1)) & (prices['High'] > prices['High'].shift(1)) & (rsi > 70)

    return signals

# Test MFI Divergence Reversal Strategy
prices = pd.read_csv("prices.csv")
signals = mfi_divergence_reversal(prices)
print(signals)
```

By identifying MFI divergences, traders can anticipate potential trend reversals.

# Special Section: Combining Momentum & Volume

## The Nature of Momentum

*Momentum is not price direction.*

Momentum is the **rate at which price changes**.

When buying pressure begins to outweigh selling pressure, price does not instantly explode. It starts by moving faster in one direction than it previously did.

This increase in speed is detectable before volume spikes become obvious.

The Momentum Oscillator captures:

- Early acceleration
- Shifts in directional force
- Changes in rate of price expansion
- Deceleration before reversals

*It responds to velocity, not crowd participation.*

# Why Acceleration Often Appears Before Volume

Participation typically follows visible movement.

Institutional positioning may begin quietly. Early accumulation does not always require large visible volume spikes. Instead, it begins with subtle directional bias.

As imbalance develops:

1. Price starts trending slightly faster.
2. Momentum shifts positive or negative.
3. Broader market participants react.
4. Volume expands in response to visible movement.

Acceleration attracts participation.

This is why, in this framework:

**Momentum identifies opportunity.**
**Volume validates conviction.**

# The Predictive Advantage of Momentum

The key strength of the Momentum Oscillator lies in its timing sensitivity.

It can detect:

- Early breakout conditions
- Developing trend shifts
- Strengthening continuation patterns
- Loss of directional force before reversals

Because it reacts to acceleration, it often signals before volume surges.

This does not make momentum "better" than volume.

It makes momentum earlier.

Early signals, however, require confirmation — and that is where volume enters.

# Volume as Validation, Not Initiation

In this book's structure, volume plays a secondary but essential role.

Momentum asks:
"Is price accelerating?"

Volume asks:
"Are participants committing to that acceleration?"

When momentum turns positive but volume remains flat, caution is required.

When momentum turns positive and volume expands, probability increases.

Volume does not initiate the signal.
It confirms whether acceleration has support.

This hierarchy prevents premature conviction.

# Establishing the Momentum → Volume Hierarchy

For this special section, the decision process follows a defined order:

1. **Structure** – Identify the market context (trend, range, breakout level).
2. **Momentum** – Detect acceleration shift.
3. **Volume** – Confirm participation strength.

Momentum leads analysis.

Volume filters conviction.

This prevents:

- Overreliance on volume spikes without direction
- Late entries caused by waiting solely for participation
- False momentum signals in illiquid environments

# Early Signal vs Confirmed Signal

It is important to distinguish between:

- A *momentum signal*
- A *tradable momentum signal*

A tradable signal requires alignment.

For example:

- Momentum crosses above zero → early acceleration signal.
- Volume expands simultaneously → confirmation.
- Structure supports breakout → high-probability setup.

*Momentum alone identifies possibility.*

*Momentum plus volume identifies probability.*

# The Risk of Ignoring Volume

Although momentum leads in this framework, ignoring volume creates vulnerability.

Acceleration without participation often results in:

- False breakouts
- Thin liquidity spikes
- Quick reversals
- Whipsaw environments

Momentum detects speed.

Volume reveals durability.

A durable move requires both.

# Strategic Implications

Placing momentum first changes execution psychology:

- Entries become earlier but structured.
- Confirmation becomes logical, not emotional.
- False signals are filtered systematically.
- Trade frequency becomes disciplined.

Instead of reacting to visible crowd behavior, the trader observes acceleration first — then waits for participation to validate.

*This improves timing without sacrificing prudence.*

# Core Principle of This Section

*Acceleration precedes expansion.*

*The market moves before the crowd commits.*

*The Momentum Oscillator captures the shift in force.
Volume determines whether that shift can sustain.*

*In this book, momentum is the engine.
Volume is the fuel gauge.*

*Without acceleration, volume lacks direction.
Without volume, acceleration lacks endurance.*

*Understanding this relationship forms the foundation for every chapter that follows in this integration section.*

# Volume as Confirmation of Momentum Breakouts

*Breakouts are acceleration events.*

*They represent the moment when price escapes compression and directional force increases. The Momentum Oscillator often detects this acceleration before price visibly clears resistance or support.*

*But acceleration alone does not guarantee expansion.*

*Volume determines whether the breakout has commitment.*

## The Anatomy of a Momentum Breakout

A momentum breakout typically unfolds in stages:

1. **Compression Phase**
    - Price consolidates.
    - Volatility contracts.
    - Momentum flattens near the centerline.
2. **Early Acceleration**
    - Momentum begins rising or falling before price breaks structure.

- Oscillator slope increases.
- Internal pressure builds.
3. **Structural Break**
    - Price clears resistance or breaks support.
    - The move becomes visible.
4. **Participation Decision**
    - Volume either expands → validation.
    - Or remains weak → vulnerability.

The trader's edge lies in recognizing stage two — but acting decisively only when stage four confirms.

---

# What Healthy Volume Expansion Looks Like

When momentum leads a breakout, volume confirmation should display:

- Clear expansion above recent average levels
- Increasing participation relative to consolidation period
- Broad candle ranges supported by sustained turnover

*Healthy volume tells you:*

*"This move is not isolated. It is accepted."*

*Momentum identifies the shift.*
*Volume confirms that others agree.*

---

## Weak Momentum Breakouts

One of the most common traps occurs when:

- Momentum spikes sharply.
- Price briefly breaks structure.
- Volume remains muted.

These breakouts often fail because:

- Liquidity is thin.
- Institutional participation is absent.
- Retail momentum chasing fades quickly.

Without volume support, acceleration becomes fragile.

Momentum without participation is often a reaction — not a trend.

# Entry Logic: Aggressive vs Confirmed

There are two structured approaches:

## 1. Aggressive Momentum Entry

- Enter when momentum crosses key thresholds.
- Anticipate breakout.
- Use smaller position size.
- Require volume expansion within 1–2 candles.

This approach prioritizes timing.

## 2. Confirmed Breakout Entry

- Wait for price to break structure.
- Confirm momentum strength.
- Require clear volume expansion.
- Enter on breakout close or shallow pullback.

This approach prioritizes durability.

Both methods rely on momentum leading — but neither ignores volume confirmation.

## Scaling into Breakouts

Volume also helps determine scaling.

- Strong momentum + explosive volume → full position size.
- Strong momentum + moderate volume → partial position.
- Strong momentum + declining volume → defensive size.

*Position sizing becomes dynamic, not static.*

*Volume does not decide direction.
It determines conviction.*

---

## Breakout Continuation vs Exhaustion

Not all high-volume momentum breakouts are continuation signals.

Watch for:

- Momentum already at extreme levels before breakout.
- Volume spike that exceeds historical norms dramatically.
- Large single-candle expansions.

When volume and momentum both spike aggressively after extended trends, exhaustion may follow.

Healthy continuation breakouts show:

- Progressive momentum expansion.
- Gradual volume build-up.
- Follow-through across multiple candles.

*Climax behavior looks explosive.*

*Continuation behavior looks sustainable.*

## Filtering False Breakouts

To avoid low-quality signals:

**Ignore breakouts when:**

- Momentum crosses threshold but slope is flattening.
- Volume is below consolidation average.
- Break occurs during illiquid sessions.

- Higher timeframe momentum contradicts direction.

Accept breakouts when:

- Momentum slope is strong and expanding.
- Volume exceeds recent baseline.
- Structure aligns across timeframes.
- Follow-through appears within 1–3 candles.

*Volume acts as the final filter.*

## The Professional Perspective

Momentum provides the early alert.

Volume answers the critical question:

"Is this move being accepted by the market?"

Professional execution does not chase acceleration blindly. It demands evidence of participation.

Momentum without volume is potential.
Momentum with volume is probability.

## Core Breakout Rule

In this integration model:

- Momentum identifies the breakout.
- Volume validates its strength.
- Structure defines the target zone.
- Risk is placed beyond invalidation.

*The trader does not trade speed alone.*

*They trade speed supported by commitment.*

# Momentum Divergence with Volume Context

*Momentum divergence occurs when price makes a new extreme, but the Momentum Oscillator fails to confirm that extreme.*

*This signals a reduction in acceleration.*

*It does **not** automatically signal reversal.*

*Divergence is a warning.*
*Volume determines whether the warning becomes actionable.*

---

## Understanding Divergence Properly

There are two primary types:

### Bullish Divergence

- Price makes a lower low.
- Momentum makes a higher low.
- Downward acceleration is weakening.

## Bearish Divergence

- Price makes a higher high.
- Momentum makes a lower high.
- Upward acceleration is weakening.

In both cases, the key concept is not direction — it is **deceleration**.

The market is still moving in the same direction.
It is simply moving with less force.

Less force can mean:

- Consolidation
- Continuation after pause
- Or reversal

  *Volume clarifies which outcome is more likely.*

---

# Divergence Without Volume Shift

If divergence forms while volume remains stable or expanding in the direction of the prevailing trend:

- The dominant side still has participation.
- The market may simply be pausing.
- Continuation remains likely.

For example:

- Price makes a higher high.
- Momentum prints a lower high.
- Volume remains strong and consistent.

This often signals slowing acceleration — not reversal.

The trend may consolidate before resuming.

Momentum weakens first.
Participation must weaken next for reversal to gain probability.

## Divergence With Declining Volume

When divergence appears alongside declining volume:

- Acceleration is weakening.
- Participation is fading.
- Conviction is eroding.

This alignment increases reversal probability significantly.

Example:

- Price pushes to new high.
- Momentum fails to confirm.
- Volume contracts during the push.

Now both force and commitment are deteriorating.

This is where professional traders begin preparing for structural breakdown.

## Volume Spike at Divergence

Another powerful scenario occurs when divergence forms and is followed by a sudden volume spike in the opposite direction.

For example:

- Bearish divergence forms at highs.
- A strong bearish candle appears.
- Volume expands aggressively.

**This signals:**

*Participation is shifting.*

*Acceleration had already warned.*
*Volume now confirms transition.*

*This is a high-probability reversal structure.*

## Filtering False Divergence

Divergence appears frequently in strong trends.

To filter noise, apply this framework:

Avoid trading divergence when:

- Higher timeframe momentum remains strongly aligned.
- Volume continues expanding with trend.
- Price structure remains clean and impulsive.

Consider acting on divergence when:

- Momentum shows clear slope deterioration.
- Volume contracts at new extremes.
- Structural support or resistance is nearby.
- Counter-directional volume expansion appears.

*Divergence is context-dependent.*

*Without context, it is noise.*

# Divergence During Ranges

In range-bound markets, divergence behaves differently.

Within a range:

- Momentum divergence near support or resistance is more reliable.
- Volume contraction toward boundaries increases reversal probability.
- Volume expansion at the opposite boundary confirms rejection.

*In ranges, divergence aligns naturally with mean reversion.*

*In trends, divergence must overcome participation strength.*

---

# Execution Framework

A structured approach to divergence trading:

1. Identify clear divergence.
2. Evaluate volume behavior at the extreme.
3. Wait for structural break or reversal candle.
4. Confirm opposing volume expansion.
5. Enter with defined risk.

*Momentum gives early warning.*
*Volume determines conviction.*

## Risk Management Implication

Divergence-based trades should:

- Use tighter stops.
- Expect initial volatility.
- Scale cautiously if volume confirmation is moderate.
- Increase size only when volume clearly shifts direction.

*Divergence trades are counter-trend early entries.*
*Volume protects against premature positioning.*

# The Core Principle

*Momentum divergence signals:*

*"The move is losing force."*

*Volume answers:*

*"Is the market withdrawing support?"*

*When both acceleration and participation decline, reversal probability increases substantially.*

*When only acceleration declines, patience is required.*

*Momentum identifies the crack.*
*Volume reveals whether the structure will break.*

# Volume Climax vs Momentum Exhaustion

*Not all strength is continuation.*

*Some strength is terminal.*

*The Momentum Oscillator measures acceleration extremes.*
*Volume reveals participation extremes.*

When both reach abnormal levels simultaneously, the market may be approaching exhaustion rather than expansion.

Understanding the difference between **healthy expansion** and **terminal climax** is critical.

---

## Momentum Exhaustion Defined

Momentum exhaustion occurs when:

- The oscillator reaches extreme overbought or oversold territory.
- The slope begins flattening.
- Successive price highs (or lows) show reduced oscillator confirmation.

*Acceleration is still positive — but no longer increasing.*

*Force is peaking.*

*This alone does not guarantee reversal.*

*Strong trends can remain extreme for extended periods.*

*This is where volume becomes decisive.*

---

## Volume Climax Defined

A volume climax is characterized by:

- A sudden spike significantly above recent averages.
- Wide price ranges.
- Emotional expansion candles.
- News-driven or panic-driven participation.

Climaxes represent crowd extremes.

They can mean:

- Final breakout acceleration.
- Or final exhaustion before reversal.

The difference depends on context.

# When Momentum Exhaustion Meets Volume Climax

The highest-probability reversal structure occurs when:

- Momentum is already stretched.
- Momentum slope begins to flatten or diverge.
- A large volume spike appears at a price extreme.
- Follow-through fails on the next candle.

This signals:

Acceleration peaked.
Participation climaxed.
Continuation failed.

That sequence often marks distribution (at highs) or accumulation (at lows).

---

# Healthy Expansion vs Terminal Spike

To distinguish continuation from exhaustion, evaluate:

### Healthy Expansion

- Momentum rising progressively.

- Volume building steadily.
- Breakout followed by continuation.
- No immediate reversal candles.

### Terminal Spike

- Momentum already extreme before breakout.
- Volume suddenly explodes after extended move.
- Large candle with long wick.
- Immediate loss of follow-through.

*Healthy moves build.*

*Climaxes erupt.*

# The Trap of Late Entry

Many traders enter aggressively at the moment of:

- Highest momentum reading.
- Largest volume spike.
- Widest candle range.

But by that stage:

Early participants are taking profit.
Late participants are entering emotionally.

*Momentum signals acceleration.*
*Volume signals participation.*

*When both reach abnormal extremes late in a move, risk increases sharply.*

*Professionals reduce exposure into climaxes — they do not initiate size blindly.*

---

## Volume Behavior After Climax

The most important confirmation comes after the spike.

Watch for:

- Reduced volume on attempted continuation.
- Immediate counter-directional volume expansion.
- Momentum rolling over from extremes.
- Failure to make new price highs or lows.

The absence of sustained participation after a spike is a warning.

*Continuation requires follow-through.*
*Exhaustion produces hesitation.*

# Reversal Timing Framework

A structured exhaustion approach:

1. Identify extreme momentum reading.
2. Observe volume spike at price extreme.
3. Wait for reversal candle or structure break.
4. Confirm opposing volume expansion.
5. Enter with defined risk beyond the extreme.

Never assume reversal solely from overbought/oversold readings.

*Extremes measure pressure.*
*Climaxes measure emotional commitment.*

*Both must align for probability to shift.*

---

# Trend Continuation Exception

Strong institutional trends may show:

- High momentum
- Elevated but stable volume
- Minor pauses
- No sharp climactic spikes

These environments represent controlled participation — not emotional climax.

*Do not mistake sustained strength for exhaustion.*

*Look for abnormality, not magnitude alone.*

## Risk Adjustment Logic

When signs of exhaustion appear:

- Reduce new long entries at highs.
- Tighten stops on open positions.
- Avoid increasing size.
- Prepare for volatility expansion.

When continuation is confirmed:

- Allow trend to extend.
- Trail stops logically.
- Avoid premature exit due to oscillator extremes alone.

*Context overrides indicator readings.*

## Core Principle

*Momentum extremes show speed.*

*Volume climaxes show emotion.*

*When speed and emotion peak simultaneously after an extended move, durability declines.*

*Acceleration attracts participation.*
*Climax often precedes transition.*

*The professional trader does not chase extremes.*
*They interpret them.*

# Pullbacks: Momentum Reset with Volume Contraction

*Strong trends do not move in straight lines.*

*They advance in impulses and retracements.*

*The professional trader does not chase impulses. They position during resets.*

In this framework:

- Momentum identifies the reset.
- Volume confirms whether the pullback is corrective or threatening.

A healthy pullback shows **declining acceleration and declining participation** — not reversal pressure.

---

## The Nature of a Momentum Reset

In a strong uptrend:

- Price pulls back toward support.
- The Momentum Oscillator declines toward the centerline.
- Momentum does not collapse into deep negative territory.

*This is not weakness.*

*It is acceleration cooling.*

*Trends require pauses to sustain structure.*

*The key question is:*

*Is this a correction — or the beginning of reversal?*

*Volume answers.*

---

## Ideal Volume Behavior During Pullbacks

A high-quality continuation pullback shows:

- Declining volume during retracement.
- Narrowing candle ranges.
- Lack of aggressive counter-trend participation.

**Volume contraction signals:**

*The opposing side lacks conviction.*

*The market is resting — not reversing.*

*When momentum begins turning upward again and volume expands in the trend direction, continuation probability rises sharply.*

---

# Warning Signs of Reversal

A pullback becomes dangerous when:

- Volume expands aggressively against the prevailing trend.
- Momentum crosses deeply beyond the centerline.
- Structural support breaks decisively.
- Counter-trend candles show wide ranges and strong closes.

Here, participation is not contracting — it is rotating.

Momentum reset becomes momentum shift.

## The Ideal Continuation Sequence

A textbook bullish continuation structure:

1. Uptrend established.
2. Momentum remains above zero for extended period.
3. Price retraces modestly.
4. Momentum declines toward zero but does not collapse.
5. Volume contracts during retracement.
6. Momentum turns upward.
7. Volume expands on breakout of pullback high.

*This sequence reflects:*

*Temporary cooling → renewed acceleration → renewed participation.*

*Momentum leads again.*
*Volume confirms again.*

# Entry Timing Framework

There are three structured pullback entries:

## 1. Early Reset Entry

- Enter as momentum flattens near centerline.
- Require visible volume contraction.
- Use smaller size.
- Add if volume expands on re-acceleration.

## 2. Confirmed Re-Acceleration Entry

- Wait for momentum to turn upward.
- Confirm volume expansion.
- Enter on break of minor resistance.

## 3. Structural Break Entry

- Wait for price to break prior swing high.
- Confirm strong volume participation.
- Enter with full defined risk.

*The choice depends on risk tolerance and timeframe.*

*Momentum defines timing.*
*Volume defines confidence.*

## Multi-Timeframe Context

Pullback quality improves significantly when:

- Higher timeframe momentum remains aligned.
- Lower timeframe momentum resets without deep divergence.
- Volume contracts on both timeframes during retracement.

When higher timeframe momentum weakens while lower timeframe pulls back, caution increases.

Continuation works best when acceleration aligns across scales.

---

## The Psychological Trap

Many traders:

- Fear entering during pullbacks.
- Interpret any downward movement as reversal.
- Exit trends prematurely at first oscillator dip.

*Understanding the momentum-volume reset structure builds confidence.*

*A pullback with declining volume is not selling pressure dominance.*

*It is absence of aggressive selling.*

*Absence of pressure is not the same as presence of opposition.*

---

## Position Sizing Logic

During pullbacks:

- Volume contraction → conservative accumulation.
- Volume stability → cautious scaling.
- Volume expansion against trend → reduce or avoid.

Once momentum re-accelerates with participation, size can increase.

Position size should expand with confirmation — not anticipation.

## Core Principle

*Strong trends breathe.*

*Momentum resets allow trends to continue.*

*Volume contraction during pullbacks signals:*

*"The opposing side lacks strength."*

*When acceleration resumes and participation returns, probability favors continuation.*

*Momentum identifies the reset.*
*Volume determines whether the reset is healthy.*

# Trend Strength: Sustained Momentum with Stable Volume

*A single momentum surge does not define a strong trend.*

*Durability defines strength.*

**True trend strength is characterized by:**

- Persistent momentum positioning.
- Stable or gradually expanding participation.
- Orderly pullbacks.
- Clean structural progression.

*Momentum reveals directional acceleration. Volume reveals whether that acceleration is being maintained.*

---

## Persistent Momentum Positioning

In strong bullish trends:

- The Momentum Oscillator remains above the zero line for extended periods.

- Pullbacks do not drive momentum deeply negative.
- Upside accelerations appear progressively.

In strong bearish trends:

- Momentum remains below zero.
- Rallies fail to produce strong positive spikes.
- Downside acceleration persists.

*The key characteristic is not extreme readings.*

*It is sustained alignment.*

*Strong trends do not constantly flip polarity.*

*They maintain directional pressure.*

---

## The Role of Stable Volume

Contrary to popular belief, strong trends do not always require explosive volume.

They require **consistent participation**.

Healthy trend volume behavior often shows:

- Moderate expansion during impulse waves.
- Contraction during pullbacks.
- Absence of erratic spikes.

- No persistent decline in participation.

*Volume stability indicates institutional commitment.*

*Erratic volume indicates emotional trading.*

*Durable trends are institutional.
Fragile moves are emotional.*

---

## When Momentum Hides Weakening Participation

Sometimes momentum appears strong while volume slowly deteriorates.

This is a subtle warning.

Signs include:

- Higher highs with progressively lower volume.
- Momentum remaining elevated but flattening.
- Narrower price expansions despite positive oscillator readings.

Here, acceleration persists — but participation declines.

*Trends can continue under these conditions, but risk increases.*

*Momentum measures force.*
*Volume measures support.*

*Force without support eventually weakens.*

---

## Identifying Trend Fragility

A strong trend becomes fragile when:

- Momentum begins producing lower highs in uptrends (or higher lows in downtrends).
- Volume declines consistently during impulse waves.
- Pullbacks show expanding counter-trend participation.
- Structure becomes overlapping and compressed.

*Fragility is gradual.*

*It does not appear in one candle.*

*This is why sustained observation matters.*

# Scaling Strategy in Strong Trends

In confirmed strong trend environments:

- Increase size during pullback resets.
- Allow wider stop placement consistent with structure.
- Trail stops logically, not emotionally.
- Avoid exiting solely due to oscillator extremes.

In weakening trends:

- Reduce size.
- Tighten stops.
- Avoid adding on marginal breakouts.
- Prepare for regime shift.

*Trend strength should influence capital allocation.*

# Momentum Drift vs Momentum Thrust

Strong trends often alternate between:

- **Momentum thrust phases** (clear acceleration).
- **Momentum drift phases** (steady, non-explosive continuation).

*Drift is not weakness.*

*Drift reflects controlled institutional movement.*

*Volume during drift phases is usually stable but not explosive.*

*Climactic spikes, in contrast, often signal transitions.*

*Understanding this difference prevents premature exits.*

# The Professional Assessment Framework

To evaluate trend strength:

1. Is momentum persistently aligned?
2. Are pullbacks shallow and controlled?
3. Is volume stable during advances?
4. Does counter-trend volume remain limited?
5. Is structural progression clean?

*If most answers are yes, trend strength remains intact.*

*If answers begin shifting, caution increases.*

---

# Core Principle

*Strong trends are not defined by intensity.*

*They are defined by durability.*

*Sustained momentum above or below the centerline reflects consistent directional force.*

*Stable volume reflects committed participation.*

*When both persist together, probability favors continuation.*

*When either begins deteriorating, risk begins rising.*

*Momentum shows the engine running.
Volume shows whether fuel remains sufficient.*

# False Momentum Signals and Volume Disconfirmation

*Not every acceleration shift deserves execution.*

*Momentum is sensitive by design.*
*Sensitivity creates opportunity — and noise.*

*False signals occur when acceleration appears briefly, but participation never commits.*

*Volume disconfirmation is the protection mechanism.*

---

## Why False Momentum Signals Occur

Momentum reacts quickly to:

- Short-term volatility spikes
- Thin liquidity movements
- News headlines
- Algorithmic bursts
- Stop runs

Because it measures rate of change, even small bursts can create oscillator crossovers or threshold breaks.

But acceleration without sustained participation rarely becomes trend.

*Speed alone does not create structure.*

---

## Low-Volume Environments

False signals are most common in:

- Illiquid trading sessions
- Holiday markets
- Low-participation consolidations
- Overnight sessions in certain asset classes

In these environments:

- Momentum may spike briefly.
- Price may break minor structure.
- Volume remains below average.

*These moves often reverse quickly.*

*When participation is thin, acceleration is unreliable.*

# The Volume Disconfirmation Rule

When momentum produces a signal, immediately ask:

"Is volume validating this shift?"

If volume:

- Expands clearly → signal strengthens.
- Remains flat → caution.
- Declines → ignore or reduce size.

Volume does not need to explode.
It needs to confirm presence.

*Acceleration without presence is unstable.*

---

# Overbought and Oversold Traps

One of the most common mistakes is reacting to:

- Momentum reaching overbought levels → immediate short.
- Momentum reaching oversold levels → immediate long.

*Extremes are common in strong trends.*

If volume remains strong in the trend direction:

- Overbought can remain overbought.
- Oversold can remain oversold.

Volume disconfirmation occurs when:

- Momentum is extreme.
- Volume contracts.
- Follow-through weakens.

*Extremes without volume shift are not reversal signals.*

*They are strength signals.*

---

# News-Driven Whipsaws

High-impact events often create:

- Sudden momentum spikes.
- Immediate structural breaks.
- Emotional price candles.

But if volume does not sustain beyond the initial reaction, the move often retraces.

In these cases:

- The first candle shows expansion.
- Subsequent candles show reduced participation.
- Momentum rolls back quickly.

*Professionals wait for sustained volume, not single-candle reactions.*

---

## Range Market False Breakouts

Within consolidation:

- Momentum may cross above zero frequently.
- Price may briefly break range boundaries.
- Volume remains muted.

*This environment produces whipsaws.*

*Volume confirmation becomes non-negotiable inside ranges.*

*Breakouts without participation inside compression structures are statistically weak.*

## Conflict Between Timeframes

False signals also appear when:

- Lower timeframe momentum accelerates.

- Higher timeframe momentum remains neutral or opposing.
- Volume does not expand across scales.

*Multi-timeframe volume confirmation improves reliability.*

*If only one timeframe shows participation, caution increases.*

## Standing Aside as a Strategy

Discipline means accepting non-alignment.

When:

- Momentum signals,
- Volume fails to confirm,

*The professional response is not forced execution.*

*It is patience.*

*Capital preservation during false environments improves long-term performance more than aggressive participation during marginal setups.*

## Structured Filtering Checklist

Before executing a momentum signal, confirm:

1. Is volume above recent average?
2. Is volume expanding in the signal direction?
3. Is higher timeframe participation aligned?
4. Is structure supportive?

*If two or more answers are no, reduce size or stand aside.*

The goal is not maximum trades.

The goal is maximum quality.

## Core Principle

*Momentum detects speed.*
*Volume confirms commitment.*

*False signals occur when speed appears without commitment.*

*Acceleration attracts attention.*
*Participation sustains movement.*

*Without participation, acceleration fades.*

*The disciplined trader does not trade movement alone.*

*They trade supported movement.*

# Momentum Regime Shifts Confirmed by Volume Rotation

*Markets do not remain in one condition indefinitely.*

They rotate between:

- Trending environments
- Ranging environments
- Accumulation phases
- Distribution phases

*Momentum reveals when directional acceleration changes.*
*Volume reveals whether capital is rotating to support that change.*

*A regime shift occurs when both align.*

# What Is a Momentum Regime Shift?

A momentum regime shift is not a single crossover.

It is a structural transition.

Examples:

- Momentum that has remained above zero for weeks begins persistently printing below zero.
- Oscillator highs gradually weaken while lows deepen.
- Acceleration flips from expansion to contraction.

*This signals a change in directional force.*

*But force alone does not confirm regime change.*

*Participation must rotate.*

## Volume Rotation Defined

Volume rotation refers to a change in participation bias.

In an uptrend:

- Bullish impulses show strong volume.
- Pullbacks show declining volume.

In a developing distribution phase:

- Bullish impulses begin showing weaker volume.
- Bearish moves begin expanding in participation.

The dominant side is losing conviction.
The opposing side is gaining presence.

That is rotation.

# Trend to Range Transition

A common regime shift occurs when:

1. Momentum extremes begin flattening.
2. Divergence appears repeatedly.
3. Volume no longer expands on new highs.
4. Pullbacks show increasing participation.
5. Structure becomes overlapping.

*The market stops accelerating.*

*Participation becomes balanced.*

*This is transition from trend to range.*

*Recognizing this early prevents trend-following strategies from overtrading in non-trending environments.*

# Range to Trend Transition

The opposite shift begins inside compression.

Signs include:

- Momentum volatility contracts.
- Oscillator remains near centerline.
- Volume gradually increases during one directional push.
- Breakout occurs with expanding participation.

*Here, acceleration emerges first.*

*Volume confirms rotation from neutrality to commitment.*

*This is the birth of trend.*

---

# The Multi-Phase Transition Model

A complete regime shift often unfolds in stages:

### Stage 1 – Momentum Warning

- Oscillator slope weakens.
- Divergence appears.
- Acceleration slows.

### Stage 2 – Volume Imbalance

- Opposing moves gain participation.
- Impulses in original direction weaken.

**Stage 3 – Structural Break**

- Key support or resistance fails.
- Price confirms transition.

> *Momentum detects early imbalance.*
> *Volume confirms capital reallocation.*
> *Structure finalizes the shift.*

# Institutional Perspective

Large participants rotate gradually.

They do not reverse positions in one candle.

You will often observe:

- Distribution at highs (heavy volume, limited progress).
- Accumulation at lows (heavy volume, limited decline).

*Momentum begins flattening during these phases.*

*Volume becomes active without directional expansion.*

> *This is preparation, not continuation.*

# Risk Management During Regime Shift

When signs of rotation appear:

- Reduce trend-following exposure.
- Avoid breakout chasing.
- Tighten trailing stops.
- Consider shorter targets.

When new regime confirms:

- Shift strategy bias.
- Increase size only after sustained participation appears.
- Align with new acceleration direction.

*Flexibility protects capital.*

*Rigidity destroys it.*

# Common Mistake: Trading Old Regimes

Many traders:

- Continue trend strategies inside emerging ranges.
- Fade range boundaries inside emerging trends.
- Ignore declining volume on breakouts.

- Ignore rising participation against trend.

*Momentum shifts first.*

*Volume rotation follows.*

*Traders who monitor both adapt faster.*

## The Alignment Rule

A true regime shift requires:

- Sustained momentum polarity change.
- Clear participation rotation.
- Structural confirmation.

*Without volume rotation, momentum shifts may be temporary.*

*Without momentum shift, volume spikes may be emotional.*

*When both align, probability shifts materially.*

## Core Principle

*Regime shifts are not events.*

*They are processes.*

*Momentum reveals directional force changing.
Volume reveals capital reallocating.*

*When force and capital rotate together, the market's character changes.*

*The disciplined trader evolves with it.*

# Strategy Alignment: Building Rules That Combine Momentum Leadership with Volume Confirmation

*Indicators do not create edge.*

*Rules create edge.*

The interaction between Momentum and Volume becomes powerful only when structured into:

- Clear entry logic
- Defined confirmation criteria
- Position sizing rules
- Exit conditions
- Regime filters

*This chapter converts interpretation into system architecture.*

# The Core Alignment Model

Every strategy built in this framework follows four stages:

1. **Acceleration Signal (Momentum)**
2. **Participation Confirmation (Volume)**
3. **Structural Validation (Price)**
4. **Risk Definition (Invalidation Level)**

*No stage replaces another.*

*Momentum without volume is anticipation.*
*Volume without momentum is noise.*
*Structure without either is random.*

*Alignment creates probability.*

---

# Step 1 – Define the Momentum Trigger

The first decision is sensitivity.

Examples of structured triggers:

- Zero-line crossover
- Break above prior momentum high
- Divergence formation

- Momentum extreme reversal
- Slope acceleration beyond threshold

Each trigger defines timing.

Higher sensitivity:

- More trades
- Lower reliability
- Requires stricter volume confirmation

Lower sensitivity:

- Fewer trades
- Higher reliability
- Allows moderate volume confirmation

*Momentum sets the tempo.*

---

# Step 2 – Define the Volume Confirmation Rule

Volume must be measurable, not subjective.

Examples:

- Current volume > 20-period average
- Volume increasing for two consecutive candles

- Breakout candle volume exceeds consolidation average
- Pullback volume below impulse volume

You may define confirmation as:

- Absolute expansion
- Relative expansion
- Contraction during correction
- Rotation during divergence

*Clarity prevents hesitation.*

---

# Step 3 – Structural Filter

Momentum and volume may align, but structure must cooperate.

Structural filters may include:

- Break of resistance/support
- Higher high / lower low confirmation
- Range boundary breakout
- Trendline break
- Retest of breakout level

*Structure defines where participation is being accepted.*

*Without structural validation, signals remain theoretical.*

## Step 4 – Position Sizing Logic

Volume strength determines size.

Example scaling model:

- Strong momentum + strong volume → full size
- Strong momentum + moderate volume → partial size
- Weak momentum + strong volume → avoid or reduce
- Strong momentum + weak volume → wait

  *This creates dynamic exposure control.*

  *Size follows confirmation.*

---

## Step 5 – Exit and Invalidation Rules

Every integrated strategy must define:

**Invalidation:**

- Opposite momentum crossover

- Structural break against position
- Volume expansion against trade

**Profit Management:**

- Momentum flattening
- Volume contraction at highs/lows
- Climax spike
- Predefined risk-reward target

*Exits must be rules-based, not emotional.*

---

# Regime-Based Strategy Selection

Different environments require different parameter sets.

In strong trends:

- Favor pullback continuation setups.
- Allow wider stops.
- Demand moderate but stable volume.

In ranges:

- Favor divergence setups.
- Demand clear volume rotation at boundaries.
- Use tighter targets.

In transitional regimes:

- Reduce size.
- Demand strong alignment before entry.

*One strategy does not fit all regimes.*

*Alignment includes environmental awareness.*

---

# Building a Repeatable Template

Every integrated strategy in this framework can follow a template:

**Market Condition:**
Describe trend/range structure.

**Momentum Condition:**
Define trigger precisely.

**Volume Condition:**
Define confirmation threshold.

**Entry Rule:**
Specify exact trigger candle.

**Stop Placement:**
Structure-based, not indicator-based.

**Position Size Rule:**
Based on volume strength.

**Exit Logic:**
Momentum or volume-based signal.

*Consistency builds statistical confidence.*

---

# Avoiding Over-Optimization

The danger in combining two indicators is complexity.

Avoid:

- Excessive parameter layering
- Too many filters
- Micromanaging every candle
- Curve-fitting historical data

*The goal is clarity, not perfection.*

*Momentum provides timing.*
*Volume provides validation.*

*Keep the structure clean.*

# The Professional Integration Mindset

Professional execution focuses on:

- Quality over frequency
- Confirmation over prediction
- Alignment over impulse
- Structure over excitement

*Momentum initiates interest.*
*Volume justifies commitment.*

*When both align within clear structural context, probability increases.*

---

# Core Principle

*A strategy is not a signal.*

*It is a structured decision process.*

*Momentum tells you when something is changing.*
*Volume tells you whether that change is supported.*

*Alignment transforms observation into action.*

# The Integrated Execution Framework: From Signal to Portfolio Discipline

*Indicators generate signals.*

*Frameworks generate consistency.*

The integration of Momentum and Volume must extend beyond single trades and influence:

- Trade selection
- Capital allocation
- Exposure management
- Risk concentration
- Psychological control

*Execution quality determines whether analytical edge becomes financial edge.*

## Step 1 – Signal Qualification

Before capital is deployed, every trade must pass qualification standards.

Minimum alignment:

1. Momentum trigger defined and clear.
2. Volume confirmation measurable and present.

3. Structure supportive.
4. Market regime identified.

*If any element is missing, size reduces or the trade is rejected.*

*Selective execution increases expectancy.*

# Step 2 – Capital Allocation Based on Confirmation Strength

Not all aligned trades are equal.

Create a graded exposure model:

### Tier A Setup

- Strong momentum expansion
- Clear volume surge
- Clean structural break
- Regime aligned

→ Full predefined risk allocation.

### Tier B Setup

- Momentum valid
- Volume moderate
- Structure acceptable

→ Reduced allocation.

**Tier C Setup**

- Momentum valid
- Weak volume confirmation

   *Observation or minimal exposure.*

   *Capital must follow quality.*

# Step 3 – Correlation Awareness

Momentum-volume signals often cluster across correlated instruments.

For example:

- Sector stocks moving together
- Currency pairs aligned to one macro theme
- Index and its components triggering simultaneously

Without discipline, this creates concentrated risk.

Portfolio-level rules:

- Limit total exposure to correlated assets.
- Avoid duplicating the same signal across multiple instruments without adjustment.

- Scale combined exposure rather than individual positions.

*Confirmation strength does not eliminate correlation risk.*

# Step 4 – Exposure Timing and Staggering

Instead of entering full exposure immediately:

- Initiate partial size on signal.
- Add if volume continues expanding.
- Add if structural continuation confirms.

*Momentum leads the first entry.*
*Volume persistence justifies expansion.*

*Scaling improves risk-adjusted performance.*

# Step 5 – Managing Trades Through Momentum Phases

Every trade moves through phases:

1. **Initiation Phase**
   - Momentum expansion
   - Volume confirmation
   - Aggressive protection required
2. **Continuation Phase**

- Stable momentum positioning
- Controlled pullbacks
- Volume contraction during retracements

3. **Maturity Phase**
    - Momentum flattening
    - Divergence potential
    - Volume spikes possible

*Position management must adapt per phase.*

*Stops tighten during maturity.*

*Aggression reduces during divergence.*

# Step 6 – Handling Conflicting Signals

Occasionally:

- Momentum remains strong.
- Volume begins deteriorating.

Or:

- Volume spikes.
- Momentum fails to follow through.

In these cases:

- Avoid increasing exposure.
- Reduce leverage.

- Shift from aggressive to defensive posture.

*Conflicts are warnings.*

*Alignment is green light.*
*Conflict is yellow light.*

## Step 7 – Performance Review Framework

To maintain edge, evaluate trades by alignment quality:

After a series of trades, review:

- Did high-volume confirmations outperform low-volume confirmations?
- Did divergence setups perform better in ranges?
- Were losses concentrated in weak participation environments?

*Refinement improves execution discipline.*

*The framework must be dynamic, not static.*

## The Psychological Dimension

Momentum triggers urgency.

Volume spikes create emotional pressure.

Without structure, traders:

- Chase breakouts late.
- Panic during pullbacks.
- Exit strong trends too early.
- Hold weakening positions too long.

*A defined framework reduces emotional decision-making.*

*Rules replace reaction.*

# The Integrated Decision Hierarchy

Every trade decision should follow this order:

1. What is the regime?
2. What is momentum signaling?
3. Is volume confirming?
4. Is structure supportive?
5. What is the risk?
6. What is the appropriate size?

*If any answer is unclear, reduce exposure.*

*Clarity precedes capital.*

# Core Principle

*Momentum provides timing.
Volume provides conviction.
Structure provides location.
Risk management provides survival.*

*The integrated framework ensures that no single signal dominates decision-making.*

*Edge is not created by indicators.*

*It is created by disciplined alignment and controlled exposure.*

**SMART MONEY**

Thank you for choosing Smart Money Publishing.

# Volume & Momentum Series

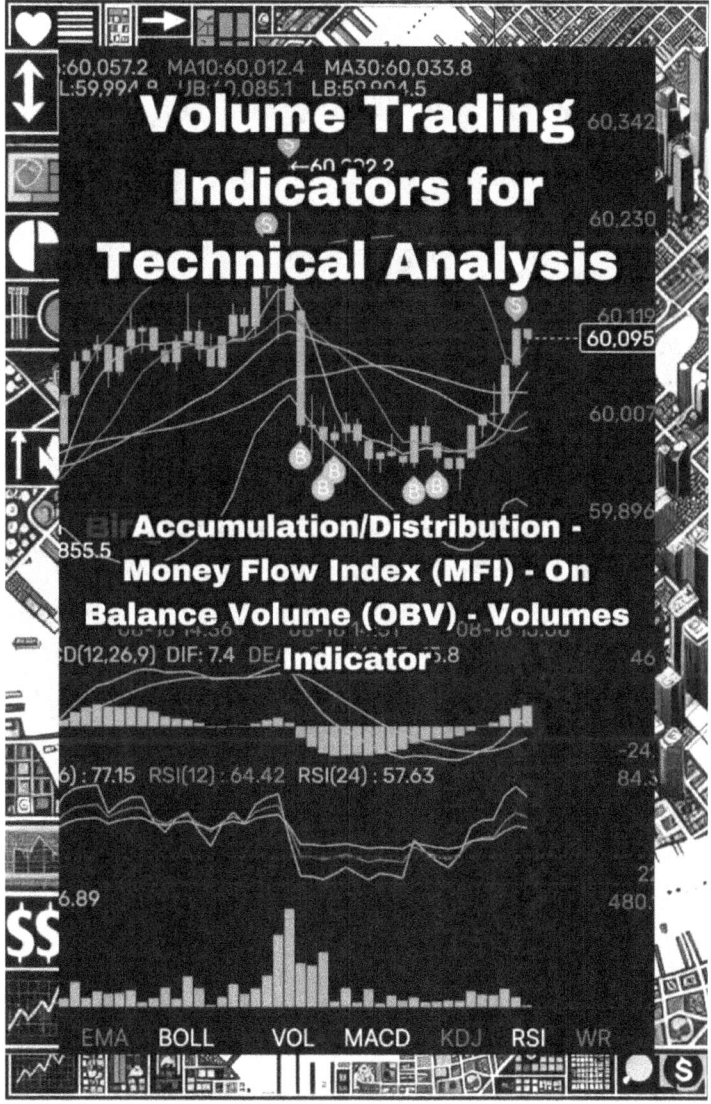

# Volume & Momentum Series

# Volume & Momentum Series

www.ingramcontent.com/pod-product-compliance
Lightning Source LLC
Chambersburg PA
CBHW052257220526
45471CB00001B/376